# What Is
# Social Media Today

# Keywords, Hashtags and You,
# Oh My!

## By
## Catherine Carrigan

Available for order through Ingram Press Catalogues

Visit my websites at
www.whatissocialmediatoday.com
www.catherinecarrigan.com
www.unlimitedenergynow.com
www.healingjewelrystore.com

Printed in the United States of America
First Printing: January 2017

ISBN: 978-0-9894506-7-6
2

# Table of Contents

# Chapter 1: Why Cinderella Doesn't Work in Business

During my 23 years in fitness, nutrition and natural healing, I have met many people who have what I call a Cinderella attitude about business.

Because they consider themselves experts in their fields – because they consider themselves to be so naturally pretty they expect everyone else to notice – they sit around waiting for their prince (the clients) to show up, thinking they don't have to do anything to make that happen.

This is an uncomfortable subject to talk about, but I'm going to talk about it anyway.

Even if Cinderella is naturally pretty, in this day and age we have Spanx, high heels, pushup bras, fake eyelashes, chronic dieting and American women alone spend about $55 billion on makeup.

And if you really want to go all out, some people spend on personal trainers, plastic surgery and Botox.

I've seen far too many friends who spent years developing their skills fail to provide a decent living for themselves because they were either unwilling or unable to master social media marketing strategy.

You can think of social media marketing as the beauty industry of business.

If you fail to present your best self to the world, nobody notices, nothing happens, and you end up with no clients and no business.

I'm a single woman. I support myself and pay my breathtaking city of Atlanta property taxes every year based on what I do and do not produce in my business.

I like to eat and I feel most comfortable remaining debt free.

When I talk to other people about social media marketing, I hear many objections:

- "It's just me in my business."

- "I don't have time."

- "I don't like Facebook."

- "I don't understand all that stuff."

- "I can pay somebody $15 an hour for that." But then the cheap person they hire doesn't actually know how, doesn't make a difference and still nothing happens, no clients show up, no students appear and no bills get paid.

To me, social media marketing is like doing my accounting.

The Internal Revenue Service does not care whether I like to do accounting.

The federal and state governments demand their money regardless of my personal opinions about them.

I don't know whether or not you have ever made any mistakes in your accounting, but I have.

I can promise you that the Georgia Department of Revenue and the Internal Revenue Service really don't care if you have a degree in accounting or business (I don't), whether you are naturally good at math or how much fun you think you aren't having while filling out all their forms.

I've learned to master what I can and get the help I need to avoid total chaos in my business.

Which brings me back to social media marketing.

As Bill Gates said, "If your business is not on the Internet, then your business will be out of business."

All businesses, no matter whether you run a tire store, are a medical intuitive healer like myself, run a yoga studio, teach hang gliding, publish books or even run a medical practice have three components:

- Production. You do your production when you write your books, see your clients, teach your yoga class.

- Administration. You work on your administration when you create the systems that keep things running.

- Sales and marketing. In this day and age, the only thing that really works is social media marketing and word of mouth.

Many people honestly believe that all they need to do to have more business is take another course, get another advanced degree or have someone else give them some sort of certificate pronouncing that they are good at what they do.

I have seen painful reminders of this fact around me for years.

In 2005, I went to England to present a series of seminars about health and wellness.

While I was there, people asked me to present a seminar to clear money issues.

As a medical intuitive healer, I clear all sorts of beliefs that hold people back, including clearing money issues.

I give all the credit for the knowledge of how to clear money issues to a woman who like me has no M.B.A. but who has run a highly successful medical intuitive healing business for decades, my mentor, Sue Maes of London, Ontario, Canada.

Sue once told me that she ended up having to clear money issues because so many people's health issues all boiled down to their lousy relationship with money.

When I was in England, I protested that I really just wanted to help everybody be healthier and happier, but when I talked to so many practitioners, a lot of them did not even own a car, much less a home. So I agreed to teach a two-day course to clear issues about money and business.

Fast forward to 2017.

Ramajon Cogan and I started What Is Social Media Today because we see what happens when people fail to market.

After five years in the book business, Rama

knows exactly what happens when authors fail to market – absolutely nothing!

When I published my second book, *What Is Healing? Awaken Your Intuitive Power for Health and Happiness*, in 2012, I had no social media presence other than a LinkedIn profile.

It wasn't enough that I wrote my book, learned how to publish it and rebuilt two websites:

www.unlimitedenergynow.com
www.catherinecarrigan.com

I also needed to learn social media marketing.

Which brings me back to another great Bill Gates quote.

"I choose a lazy person to do a hard job. Because a lazy person will find an easy way to do it."

Ramajon Cogan and I have been working to create a system so simple that once you put it

together, you can practice it every day to rocket your business to the next level.
What is social media today?

Social media today happens when you finally stop avoiding the issue and embrace the concept that putting your best self forward in the world is actually fun and easy.

Just like Cinderella feels fabulous when she steps out of the ashes to put on her princess outfit, so too can you feel amazing when you find a way to create a social media strategy that works for you and your business.

## Chapter 2: The 5 Stages of Change in Social Media

There's a distinct psychological process that you go through in the  five  stages of change in social media today.

You can't begin to win the Game of Social Media until you have gone through this process in your head, so I want to explain to you what this process is.

The more you understand your own psychological process, the quicker you can move from the stage of precontemplation to winning the Game of Social Media with ease and grace.

Hi, my name is Catherine Carrigan.

I don't have an M.B.A. or a marketing degree.
I'm a single woman running a home-based business in Atlanta, Georgia.

Here's why I can help you walk through your own process so that you can go from avoiding the subject all together to winning the Game of Social Media.

My Klout score – a measure of overall social media influence – is 68.

Once your Klout score is over 60, you are in the top 5 percent of social media influencers.

For well over a year now, I've been in the Top 100 Twitter users in Atlanta, Georgia, compiled by Evan Carmichael.

I'm a medical intuitive healer and the author of five books.

Because I can work by phone or Skype with clients all over the world as a medical intuitive, I consider myself to have an international business.

Indeed, not only do I work every week with clients all over the U.S. and the U.K., over the years I have also worked with clients in Australia, India, Saudi Arabia, Kenya and Hong Kong.

Being able to reach potential customers and readers among the 2.1 billion people in the world who have a social media account is part of why I take my marketing in social media so very seriously.

By playing to win the Game of Social Media, I no longer have to rely on any of the 5.7 million people in Atlanta willing to push their way through the 12th worst traffic in the U.S. to come and work with me in person.

I can simply sit on my sofa, put on my yoga toe

stretchers and drink a cup of tea while turning on my Skype to go to work.

I am a Phi Beta Kappa graduate of Brown University but, as I will explain in a moment, until a few years ago I understood so little about computers, the internet and marketing I actually broke my Apple desktop computer because I had been turning it off incorrectly every day for the previous four years.

The metrics about where I stand in social media are interesting, but the metric that is most impressive to me personally is the fact that when I checked my accounting, my gross revenues for the first six months of 2016 went up 50 percent over the same period of 2015.

Ramajon Cogan and I want to teach you not only how to win the Game of Social Media, we want to teach you how to succeed in your business – whether that be to sell more books, get more clients or make more money.

I attribute 100 percent of my recent success in my business to the fact that I like to play the Game of Social Media and have figured out how to win.

So what are the 5 stages of change you go through when you want to win the Game of Social Media?

- **Precontemplation.** During this stage, you think that the cons of doing anything about social media campaigns outweigh the pros.

- **Contemplation.** When you go through this step, you may consider social media training, but the cons still outweigh the benefits of social media so you do nothing.

- **Planning.** At this stage, you set up a social media strategy template. This is what Rama and I will be teaching you when you sign up to work with us at www.whatissocialmediatoday.com.

- **Action.** Finally, you are moving forward. You may not be a social media specialist or a social media manager, but you are playing the Game of Social Media.

- **Maintenance.** You play the Game of Social Media consistently and have integrated social media into your daily life.

Now here's the thing.

Each of these stages of change occurs between your ears.

Learning to win the Game of Social Media is psychological and a matter of education.

In other words, this process is both emotional and mental.

In my work as a medical intuitive, I read the five bodies – the physical body, the energy body, the emotional, mental and spiritual bodies. Of all of these resolving the issues in your emotional body is always the most important.

I've heard all the excuses:

- I don't have time.

- I tried Twitter for two days and it didn't work.

- I don't want to talk about my personal life in public.

- I can hire someone for that. According to our search engine optimization expert, Scott D. Smith of London, England, if you actually hired someone who knew what they were doing, it would cost you about 4,000 English pounds per month.

You may already have a Facebook account, a Twitter account, an Instagram or be uploading videos on Youtube but here's the truth – unless or until you create a social media strategy where you are clear about your own brand identity, you probably aren't getting anywhere.

Even if you are willing, if you fail to plan, you can bet that sooner or later you will drop back to either precontemplation or contemplation because you aren't getting new customers, new readers or more money and you will feel very frustrated.

"I tweeted for two whole days and nothing happened," you may say to yourself. "This stuff doesn't work! What's the point?"

Now let me drill this down for you.

The more you can understand what's going on between your ears, the more likely you will be to win the Game of Social Media.

Rama and I sincerely want to empower you to win this game, and that's why we set up this business. We believe that people all over the world want to win the Game of Social Media but simply don't know how.

**Precontemplation.** Let me use myself as an example. In 2011, I got a divorce. Within a two week period, I had what I refer to in healing work as the blessing of a breakdown. Everything broke all at once so I had no choice but to fix it. My cellphone broke and then my desktop computer broke. I found myself weeping at the Apple store because I knew nothing about computers. Feeling very overwhelmed and helpless, I signed up for the Apple One to One program. I would go to the Apple store to take lessons (unfortunately Apple has phased out this program) and whenever one of my devices would break down, which seemed to happen practically all the time. At that point, I discovered that the reason my computer broke was that I had been turning it off incorrectly every day for four years. I had heard remotely about Facebook and Twitter but didn't have any idea why anybody would waste their time blathering on in front of people they had never met.

If you have ever gone through a divorce, you know how rough that can be. At one point, somebody sent me an email explaining to me that I was "under the influence of the devil," quote unquote. "Who knew?" I thought. I was very thankful not to be on social media at all because I was having enough of a hard time handling all the pressure of change. Like many people, at that point in my life I had an actual fear of social media.

**If YOU are in the precontemplation stage,** more than likely you have loads of excuses about why you won't do social media – you're too busy, you think you can just hire that out – which by the way, is a terrible idea and ultimately won't work – either you can't or won't be bothered. You may not be making much money in your business or not selling any of the books you worked so hard to write and publish, but mentally and emotionally you have checked out.

**Contemplation.** At the Apple store they taught me how to build my first blog. The reason I did this is a friend at the time convinced me by saying that although I am good at many things, my skills as a medical intuitive healer are off the chart and can not be learned or taught. She said I should create a website to start talking about my work as a medical intuitive healer so that people can understand how I can help them. Because I had heard that you had to pay money if you used other people's photos on your website, I started taking photos of my orchids and my garden with my iPhone so that I would have free photos. I kept hearing about social media, but it was all I could do to run my business and set up my new blog in addition to running a website I had owned for many years and writing my monthly newsletter.

**If YOU are in the contemplation stage**, more than likely you are either new to running a website or blog and you haven't figured out how to get people to start actually visiting your website. You may not even be aware how you can check to see if people are visiting your website. You don't know how to market your content through the social media. You probably don't have many people visiting your website and you adopt the hope and pray approach, hoping and praying people might happen to notice what you have worked so hard to put up on the internet. But the idea of engaging in social media still feels a bit daunting.

**Planning.** Now this is a huge shift.

I have spent several years in the planning stage, learning about how to present myself, figuring out which hashtags are most effective for attracting the most business. For example, when I write too much about gardening and orchids, I notice that my business drops off slightly. But when I blog about my work as a medical intuitive healer, all of a sudden I get calls and emails from people all over the world. I have a plan not just for actually writing a blog but for promoting what I have written on eight different social media sites – Facebook, Twitter, Pinterest, Goodreads, Tumblr, Google+, LinkedIn and Instagram. Every blog I write gets posted not only on eight different social media sites but distributed through a dashboard, usually with 8 to 12 different headlines and a photograph blasting out once an hour.

**If YOU are in the planning stage**, you are about to sign up for our new program! You have realized that your haphazard approach to social media isn't working. You realize you have to figure out what you want to be known for, what your ideal hashtags are and have a strategy for creating content. You want to brand your blog and figure out a way to attract people to your books, your website and your business.

**Action**. Even though I have a lot of energy and am highly motivated, I don't maintain a rigid schedule of creating content. I generally meditate first thing in the morning and then write. Frankly I do everything intuitively, including my business, and often wait for guidance about what to write about. For example, in January my intuition told me to write articles about healing for the knees. One of these articles had 6,600 visitors in a single month! Once I write, I then do what the experts call SMO – social media optimization. I then optimize my content to be distributed throughout the social media. While in action, I focus on building relationships, not just selling. I focus on giving value by offering content that people need and want.

**If YOU are in action**, YOU'RE FINALLY PLAYING THE GAME OF SOCIAL MEDIA! Yea! You know what your brand is, you know your hashtags and you have discovered a rhythm for creating and distributing content throughout your social media platform. You do not sell, sell sell, you connect, connect, connect. Your ideal ratio of offering helpful content to asking people to buy your stuff is ideally about 20 to 1.

Most people would never go to a party and ask everybody in the room to buy their stuff. You no longer act like a social media idiot. Instead of telling everybody all day long to buy your stuff, you make friends, you interact, you share and when you finally have something wonderful to say or sell everybody else shares it for you because they like you. People buy from other people they like and you have learned how to be likable in public.

**Maintenance.** I have discovered a rhythm that works for me. I actually enjoy creating content. I keep my iPhone with me and photograph beautiful flowers on my walks. I admit I am a bit obsessive about photographing my orchids and garden in their various stages of change. I listen to my clients' concerns and write articles that discuss how to solve their problems. In addition to running my social media accounts, I write a monthly newsletter that gets emailed out and then promoted through my social media channels. None of this feels overwhelming. I have FUN doing it! It's even more fun when I go to my Quickbooks and realize that my hard work of figuring out how to win the Game of Social Media is paying off!

**If YOU are in maintenance**, you have created a brand for yourself, you have a content creation schedule, you deliver to your social media platform regularly and you are having FUN. Your audience for your books and business grows day by day and month by month. You make more money, help more people and are able to make a bigger impact because more people understand how you can help them.

If you recognize that you are stuck in one of these stages of change, call today to learn how you too can win the Game of Social Media.

Among social media marketing companies, what sets us apart and makes our program unique at http://whatissocialmediatoday.com
is that we understand that this is a psychological process.

By understanding what stage of change you are in, you can move to the next step and have fun playing the Game of Social Media with us.

# Chapter 3: Benefits of Social Media for 5 Kinds of Entrepreneurs

Although we can all benefit in multiple ways from the 2.1 billion people on the planet who have a social media account, the benefits of social media are crucial today for five kinds of entrepreneurs:

- The solopreneur

- The mompreneur

- The ompreneur

- The authorpreneur

- The infopreneur

If you are a solopreneur, mompreneur, ompreneur, authorpreneur or infopreneur, your online audience is the most valuable asset to the long-term success of your business.

If you fall into any of these categories, sign up today to work with:

Ramajon Cogan and Catherine Carrigan
www.whatissocialmediatoday.com.

We can show you how to share your intention globally using the power of social media.
Who are these people and are you one of them?

- **The solopreneur** is a person who runs their own business. If this is you, you do everything – you run the production, the sales and marketing and all your own accounting. You take the trash out, return your own phone calls, make your schedule in between fixing meals, going for a bike ride or a walk and dropping your kids to soccer practice. You may run a home-based business, a coaching practice, operate a company part time in addition to holding down a regular job as an employee of a corporation or sell products through a multi-level company.

- **The mompreneur** is a woman who does it all – the kids, the washing, ironing, shopping, cooking and oh yes running a business. If this is you, not only are you more than likely a solopreneur you are also the chief psychologist and overburdened personal assistant for your kids, pets and possibly aging parents. There's a lot on your plate and you would like to keep yourself on the to-do list also.

- **The ompreneur** is a person who runs a mind-body wellness business. You may operate a small yoga, tai chi, qi gong or Pilates studio, teach meditation classes, offer coaching, astrology readings, Reiki, energy healing, medical intuitive healing or other services that empower others to make a deeper mind-body connection. If this is you, you are working hard to keep your own mind and body balanced while managing to make a living.

- **The authorpreneur** is a person who writes books. If this is you, you may be on your first book or have a well-established brand through a series of books you have created on specific topics. You may be retired or write books on the side while working full-time as an employee of a corporation or in your own solopreneur business. If this is you, you are looking to connect to the kind of people who would like to buy your books and possibly other related products and courses you create.

- **The infopreneur** is a person who sells information. If this is you, you may be running a webinar or live seminar business, offering CDs, audio download recordings or other kinds of internet downloads or live in person trainings. You create content that you are wanting to sell to a large audience. You could teach people how to paint their house, how to cook, how to run marathons more successfully or cover many other topics.

From an energetic perspective, the collective consciousness now manifests through social media.

This is now known as the Virtual Collective Consciousness.

VCC occurs when a large group of persons, brought together by a social media platform think and act with one mind and share collective emotions

When you put a message out, the effects ripple out into the world and then come back to you.

You have 7 seconds to grab a person's attention when they visit your website.

Do you have what it takes not only to draw attention to you and your business but to build an audience that will support you financially for the rest of your life?

Here's how each of these social networks can help you:

- **Facebook.** Through Facebook, you can connect to thousands of groups of like-minded people through its 1.1 billion unique monthly visitors. Not only does Facebook allow you to keep up with what your friends are doing, you can share your blog articles, send out coupons, run contests, do informal surveys and let everybody know when you launch a new product or service or publish your latest book. You can stream live video events. You can have not only a personal page but also a Facebook page for your business.

Through Facebook, you can keep up with people you already know and grow your fan base. Here you can reach 72 percent of adult internet users.

- **Twitter.** Twitter is the ultimate generator for in-bound marketing with 310 million unique monthly visitors. Here you can connect to a world of people you have never met but with whom you have mutual interests. Through the effective use of hashtags, you can sort out not only what you are looking for but other people who can buy your services and products can find you. You drive people to your website through the use of shortened links in your tweets and in your branded use of photographs, videos and other images. You can live-tweet your events to let everybody know what's happening.

- **Youtube.** After Google, Youtube is the second largest search engine with more than 3 billion searches a month. By making short videos about the benefits of your service or product, you can not only inform the public about what you have to offer you can grow an enormous following. You do not have to hire a Hollywood producer, your iPhone or Android phone will work just fine. You don't need to be hired by radio or TV to run your own show, you can record your own video through your phone or videoconferencing services like Zoom.us and develop a huge following.

- **LinkedIn.** Not only can you post your resume online through LinkedIn, you can accumulate personal endorsements for each of your skill sets. You can post your blog on LinkedIn, which can allow you to reach a wider audience than you may be able to reach through your website alone. You can join LinkedIn groups to get ideas about how to solve problems in your business as well as to promote what you do to the 225 million people every month who visit LinkedIn.

- **Pinterest.** You can post photographs of each of your products or services on Pinterest, which is fastest growing social network along with Tumblr. Each photo you post can contain a direct link to drive other users to your website where you can sell it. This is a great place to showcase arts, crafts, fashion, interior design, do it yourself projects and how-to information. You can create boards on topics that you want to be known as an expert about and invite other people to contribute to group boards, thereby creating a like-minded community. If you are stumped or bored, you can get inspired with new ideas by the 250 million people a month posting on Pinterest. Because the majority of Pinterest users are women, you can connect easily here to a large female audience.

- **Instagram.** Here you can post photos and videos of your products and services and build the image of your brand. By incorporating links back to your website with each post and multiple hashtags, you can quickly reach an unlimited audience looking for what you have to offer. This is the ideal place to connect with young adults as 55% of online adults ages 18 to 29 use Instagram. You offer a behind-the-scenes look at you and your business to the 100 million people a month who visit Instagram.

- **Google+.** Posting articles on Google+ immediately feeds your information into Google, the largest search engine in the world. Posting your blogs here can help you get to the first page of Google, which is marketing gold as 91 percent of people searching do not go beyond page one of Google. In addition, you can offer Google hangouts to meet with customers and clients from all over the world. Like Facebook, you can connect with Google+ groups of like-minded people to share ideas, get inspired or promote your products and services.

- **Tumblr.** Tumblr offers you a FREE blog where you can post images and information about your products and services. If you are just starting out and do not have the money to create your own blog or website, Tumblr would be a great place for you to start. Even if you have not heard of it, 110 million people visit Tumblr every month.

- **Goodreads.** Goodreads is the world's largest social media network for readers and authors. Like LinkedIn, you can repost your blog here if you have an author page. You can run giveaways to promote your latest book and connect with people who actually read and buy books, receive reviews and find out more about the current business of writing, publishing and marketing books.

What's so great about these social networks from the point of view of an entrepreneur:

1.  You don't have to spend money to market to billions of people. You just have to spend time creating quality content that other people will want to share, comment on, view and click on.

2.  You can easily connect with like-minded people who will appreciate your products and services.

3.  By creating content through your website or blog that you share through the social networks, your website will end up ranking higher on the search engines.

4.  Google has changed its algorithms to try to outsmart the SEO (search engine optimization) experts that big companies hired to try to rank higher. Nowadays if you want your business to rank high in the search engines, you have to be popular in

the social media.

5. Even the SEO experts recommend SMO – Social Media Optimization – to support the work they do on the back end of your website so that you can show up in searches for your products and services.

6. You can connect with social media influencers who will be happy to share your ideas, content, product or services. These people are mavens with thousands up to millions of followers who heed their advice.

7. Many experts now believe that social media is the biggest influencer of buying decisions as 4 in 10 social media users have purchased an item after sharing it or marking it as a favorite on Facebook, Twitter or Pinterest.

8. 74% of consumers rely on social media to inform their purchasing decisions.

9. Only 33 percent of consumers trust ads these days but 90 percent trust peer recommendations.

10. By carefully researching topics and hashtags, you can create images and content that become wildly popular, contributing to viral marketing where thousands of people click through to your website where they will ultimately become your consumers and adoring fans.

11. You can generate positive word of mouth that can spread fast on the internet. 58% of consumers share positive experiences and seek advice from friends and family when they talk about brands on social media.

12. 43% of consumers are more likely to buy a new product when learning about it on social media.

13. 30% of consumers learn about products

from friends or personal social media accounts.

The blessing of all this is that you no longer have to spend money purchasing radio, TV, newspaper or magazine ads to market your business.

You no longer have to hire a PR agency, Madison Avenue advertising company, literary or talent agent or other media representative.

All you really have to do is learn how to market yourself and your business effectively through social media.

# Chapter 4: How I Helped My Brother Get to Page 1 of Google

Recently my brother Dr. Richard Schulze Jr. posted an article on his blog that immediately went to Page 1 of Google.

Like many solopreneurs, my brother works in a highly competitive industry.

He is an ophthalmologist in a solo practice in Savannah, Georgia. His main competitors work in groups. These groups are supported by area hospitals and work as a team to grab as large a share of the market as they can.

To survive, my brother has had to embrace  social media strategy.

It's not enough that he's a *magna cum laude* graduate of Princeton University, that he went on to study English literature at Oxford University before receiving his M. Phil. degree and graduating with his M.D. from the University of Virginia in 1990.

It's not enough that he performed his internship at Roanoke Memorial Hospital in Virginia before moving on to his residency in ophthalmology at the Ochsner Clinic in New Orleans.

It's not enough that he's such a great doctor that he helped me get rid of migraine headaches by figuring out the precise prescription for reading glasses.

No, being smart, well-educated or an excellent practitioner these days just won't cut it.

Getting to page 1 of Google is marketing gold because 90 percent of searchers don't go past page 1.

On top of that, if you are able to create original content that shows up on page 1 of Google, you are going to receive 90 percent of the clicks once people land there.

All this translates into more people going to your website, which means more fans and followers and ultimately customers who pay you money to do what you love to do.

No matter what your industry, you've got to master social media strategy to survive.

This is the strategy that Ramajon Cogan and I plan to teach you when you sign up for our program at www.whatissocialmediatoday.com

One day recently my brother and I were sitting down on the porch of my mother's house in Savannah.

I brought out my laptop and I was showing him what I was doing to promote my work at my two websites www.catherinecarrigan.com and www.unlimitedenergynow.com.

While I was in the process of writing, publishing and taking four recent books to No. 1 on Amazon, I began to develop a social network and over a period of time developed a social media strategy.

Part of that strategy begins with two simple steps:

1. Set up a website with WordPress. That's because WordPress has an awesome plugin called Jetpack that allows you to blast all the articles you create to each and every single one of your social media accounts.

2. Set up a Google+ account. Google+ has many terrific features. Even if you never

take advantage of the majority of them, you need to understand one simple fact. Google+ feeds into Google, the largest search engine in the world. When you write a blog and your Jetpack blasts that link over to Google+ voila, you are in marketing heaven.

Of course, I gave my brother a whole bunch of other pointers.

Given that my brother wrote a great article, I helped him with SMO – social media optimization. Practically every hour today a link to his fabulous content will be circulating through Facebook, Twitter, LinkedIn, Google+, Tumblr and Pinterest. Yesterday I posted his content on Goodreads and LinkedIn.

But he himself had already gotten to Page 1 of Google.

That's what brothers and sisters are for – to help each other out.

What is social media today? Social media today happens when you learn from the people around you who are already successful with social media strategy.

# Chapter 5: Begin With Your Keywords

Scott D. Smith, our very excellent SEO search engine optimization expert at http://www.scottdsmith.co.uk, says that knowing, understanding and using your keywords are the most important steps you can take to get found on the internet.
So what is a keyword?

A keyword is a word or phrase that people type in to search engines such as Google, Bing, Yahoo, ask.com, Baidu, Excite, DuckDuckGo, AOL and others to find what they need.

The internet is a huge place.

When you find the right keywords, you make it easier for potential customers to find you.
Even if you are an expert at what you do, if you do not know your keywords and use them in all your marketing, you may lose market share to more savvy competitors.

You can search for keywords at these free tools:

Google Adwords Keyword Tool
https://adwords.google.com/KeywordPlanner

Wordtracker
https://freekeywords.wordtracker.com

Google Trends
https://www.google.com/trends/

Ubersuggest
http://ubersuggest.org/

SEOBook

http://tools.seobook.com/keyword
tools/seobook/

WordStream
http://www.wordstream.com/keywords/

Keywordtool-io
http://keywordtool.io/

BuzzSumo    http://buzzsumo.com/

http://www.InstaKeywords.com

Go to these websites, plug in the words or phrases that you think people are most likely to use when searching for your products and services.

You will get a better idea of how to present yourself once you narrow down your top keywords.

At What Is Social Media Today, we help you

identify your top keywords as part of our digital social strategy.

Knowing your keywords helps you brand yourself through the social media and prepares the way for you to come up with your hashtags.

Here's the bottom line: Keywords are crucial. Learn your keywords. Memorize them. Emblazon them in your brain.

Then use your keywords everywhere you communicate through the social media so that you present a consistent and successful digital social signature.

If you don't know your keywords, you really won't know exactly who you are and you will have trouble winning what we call the Game of Social Media.

# Chapter 6: What The Heck Is A Hashtag?

If a tree falls in the social media without a hashtag, does anybody hear it?

And if nobody knows about it will the fact that the tree fell be shared?

The answer to both questions is NO, not likely, which is why Ramajon Cogan and I want YOU to know more about hashtags.

Your immediate circle of friends or anyone watching your Instagram or Twitter feed that second may see your post but then what you just may have spent hours creating or curating gets lost in the flow.

A hashtag is a word or group of words preceded by a pound sign.

Hashtags are searchable terms throughout the social media.

If you see them on Facebook and Twitter, hashtags usually show up in a different color than regular text.

If you click on a hashtag within the body of a message, you will be automatically led to a host of other messages all talking about the same topic.

If you want to win the Game of Social Media, part of what you will need to do is wrap your head around hashtags.

These coded words and phrases have become of utmost importance because if you fail to use a hashtag, the message you post becomes lost in the verbal clutter.

For example, on Facebook, the largest social network, 31.25 messages get sent out every MINUTE!

How is anything you're going to say going to end up being found by a community of like-minded people if you don't have a way to hashtag?

On Twitter, people send out 347,222 messages a minute.

Think what you have to say is important?

Then you'd better find a way to make your message get discovered, catalogue and shared.

On Instagram, where users typically post the most hashtags of any social media site since Instagram allows up to 30 hashtags per post, 48,611 photos get posted per minute.

So how do you discover which hashtags are right for you?

A good place to start is Hashtagify.me.
Looking up hashtags on Hashtagify.me is like playing a word association game.

Let's say you're going to use the hashtag #author.

Today #author has a Hashtagify.me rank of 67.9, which means that it's a pretty popular hashtag and a lot of people are talking about that subject.

You want the hashtags you choose to rank as high as possible because that means lots of people all over the world are looking for information about that topic and are more likely to be interested in what you have to say.

If you plug #author into the Hashtagify.me search box, you'll find a host of related terms that show up – for example, writer, book, am writing, am reading, writing, and so on.

This gives you a clue as to other hashtags you can use so that other people who are interested in this topic can find your message.

Another interesting feature of Hashtagify.me is that if you look at the top menu, you will discover "Top Influencers."

If you click on that button, you will be automatically led to a list of the top Twitter users who speak about that topic.

Influencers are key individuals in the social media who have built up a significant following.

Once you identify key influencers who are using the same hashtags as you, you may want to form a relationship with them in a win-win way so that you share each other's messages.

In this way you can quickly build an online community to support you and your business for years to come.

What is social media today? Social media today happens when you rock hashtags, developing a worldwide audience of people who are just as passionate as you about a specific topic.

# Chapter 7: The Top 7 Responsibilities of a Social Media Manager

Whether you are a solopreneur who needs to market your small business or you head the marketing department of a billion dollar corporation, there are 7 crucial responsibilities for a social media manager.

1. Create content around your keywords and hashtags.

2. Curate content from other people who talk about your keywords and hashtags.

3. Post.

4. Schedule future posts.
5. Measure your success.

6. Respond.

7. Plan.

As you embrace all aspects, you can learn how to win the Game of Social Media that Ramajon Cogan and I have been talking about here at What Is Social Media Today.

1. Create content around your keywords and hashtags. Blog. Create videos. Take photographs. Make graphics. Once you know the keywords that people will be looking for when they search for your business, books, services and products, how many ways can you create content that tells your story that other people will find so awe inspiring they want to share?

2. Curate content that illustrates your keywords and hashtags. You don't have to create everything you post. You can comb through the social media and internet to find content that your followers will find relevant, amusing and helpful. Share this information and gain the trust of your fans and the appreciation of the folks who created that content. The more you share the work of others, the more likely others will be willing to share your content.

3. Post. Once you have created great content, spread your links throughout the social media. How many social media sites can you find that would be willing to share your information? The more places your information gets posted, the more likely you are to increase the number of people visiting your website and ultimately buying your products and services and the more well-known you will become as an expert on your keywords and hashtags.

4. Schedule future posts. Once you have created content, you can schedule it out to be posted not just today but on a daily, weekly and/or monthly basis. You can use services like Hootsuite to schedule your posts.

5. Measure your success. You can visit Google Analytics to discover how many people are coming to your website from the social media. Pay attention to what content you create or curate that gets the most likes and the most shares. Notice if your fans are actually coming for your keywords and hashtags or if they are looking for something else. Adjust your strategy according..

6. Respond. Once you post, people will be responding to what you had to say. Social media is – get this – social. It's not enough to engage in a one-way conversation. Respond to people who like and share your

information. Get in on the conversation. As you do this, you will build loyalty, trustworthiness and appreciation.

7. Plan. Think ahead. What are you going to create or curate over the next few days, weeks and months to tell the story of your keywords and hashtags? How can you be consistent, maintaining a posting schedule you can keep up with?

# Chapter 7: Top Kinds of Content a Social Media Manager Can Create

As a social media manager, once you have identified the keywords and hashtags that will help your customers find you through the search engines, you can create content to attract them.

What kind of content can you create to attract your customers?

- Blogs. Write blogs between 500 and 2,500 words that tell the story of your products, books, business and services. Writing a blog that you share with your social media network is one of the best ways to draw people back to your website. Post the link to your blog in as many places as you can throughout the social media.

- Photographs. Use your smart phone to take photographs that tell your story. Colored visuals increase people's willingness to read a piece of content by 80 percent.

- Videos. Use your smart phone to make videos that you post to your blog and social media sites. 51.9 percent of marketing professionals name video as the kind of content with the best return on investment.

- Livestreaming. The top live streaming social media sites include Youtube, Facebook, Google+, Meerkat and Periscope. You can create live video events and invite your tribe to participate.

- Graphics. You can use sites like canva.com

to create graphics integrating words and pictures.

- Infographics. Create images that integrate statistics, facts and images. Infographics are shared on social media 3 times more than any other type of content. FREE sites that allow you to create infographics include easely.ly and piktochart.com.

- GIFs, or Graphic Interchange Format. These are image files that are compressed to reduce transfer time that move without sound, for example, a rotating globe.

- Quotes. You can collect inspiring quotes to share with your tribe. You can share your own quotes or use sites like Goodreads or Brainyquote to find inspiring quotes your audience might like.

- Surveys. You can create lists of questions to inspire audience participation. You can create FREE basic surveys with sites like surveymonkey.com.

- Newsletters. A regular newsletter can be distributed through your social media channels. Email marketing companies like Constantcontact.com to create email newsletters that you then post on social media.

- Event updates. Give your tribe updates on what is going on with your business, book or products.

- Recommendations. Based on your experience, you can recommend products or services that your tribe might like.

- Giveaways and contests. You can give away a book, product or service in a contest. For example, Goodreads allows authors to offer a giveaway of your book, thereby marketing the news about your book to potential readers.

- Testimonials. Post comments from happy customers with links to the products and services that they enjoyed the most.

- Opinions. Share your opinions on current events.

- Status updates. Post where you are and what you are doing. For example, if you teach a regular class, post your whereabouts to promote your event.

# Chapter 8: 7 Steps to Build Your Tribe in Social Media

Seth Godin, author of the book *Tribes,* defines a tribe this way:

"A tribe is a group of people connected to one another, connected to a leader, and connected to an idea."

The larger and more committed your tribe, the more successful you will be:

- If you are an *entrepreneur,* building a tribe is essential to the sale of your product or service.

- If you are an *ompreneur,* building a tribe allows you to share your ideas of mind-body wellness.
- If you are a *mompreneur,* building your tribe helps you reach outside your home and family.

- If you are an *authorpreneur,* building your tribe empowers you to sell more books.

- If you are a *solopreneur,* building your tribe is crucial to creating a referral network.

The larger and more committed your social network, the easier it will be for you to win the Game of Social Media.

Once you know your keywords and hashtags, follow these seven simple steps to build your tribe:

1. Hashtags can help you find the folks who

share the same obsessions, professions, products and services. You can find these fellow tribe members by searching hashtags on Twitter, Facebook, Pinterest and all the other social media channels.

2.  Go to Klout to find other people in your same profession. Put in your keywords and hashtags in the search box. Klout gives you great feedback to show you how well you are doing in the social media. Here you can compare yourself with others and discover the folks who are talking about your same topics.

3.  Go to Google+ and use your keywords and hashtags to find communities. Google+ feeds Google, the No. 1 search engine in the world, so participating in communities in Google+ may help you boost your ranking in the top search engine. Just like Facebook has groups, Google+ has communities that may have hundreds of thousands of members all talking about

your topics. You can share your blog articles with more people and direct potentially hundreds of thousands of people over to your website.

4. Build your own tribe by creating your own Facebook group with your keywords and hashtags. Our client Bill Murphy did just this by setting up a Facebook group called The Metaphysical Trader. He's going to be attracting people who are interested in the integration of spirituality and business. If you don't want to create your own Facebook group, join an existing group that focuses on your hashtags and keywords.

5. Look to meet people in real life with the same interests. Go to meetup.com, plug in your keywords and hashtags to find people in your local area.

6. Support the wingmen who share, like and retweet your information. These people are your tribe even if they are not using the

exact same keywords or hashtags. If someone is constantly sharing or retweeting your information, they are more than likely a like-minded person. Make a list of people who are your top supporters and share their information regularly. You are going to be most successful playing the Game of Social Media by being generous.

7. Create a monthly newsletter based on your keywords and hashtags to channel your social media followers into becoming paying customers. Once they become your newsletter subscriber, these are your most raving fans who are likely to become your customers, readers and purchases of your products. This is marketing gold. Have a button on your website that shows people how to sign up for your newsletter.

## Chapter 9: Want to Learn More About How to Win the Game of Social Media?

Join us at

[http://whatissocialmediatoday.com/the-program/](http://whatissocialmediatoday.com/the-program/).

There are three ways you will be learning:

- One-on-one training

- Webinars

- Playing the Game of Social Media with others

1. Module 1: Assessment. We'll take a look at where you are with your social media, your website and your branding.

2. Module 2: Setup. We'll be walking you through the steps to set yourself up for success.

3. Module 3: Content Creation. Learn how to create content to draw people to your website where they can learn about your books, products, business and services.

4. Module 4: Win the Game of Social Media. Learn the ins and outs of the key social media platforms.

5. Module 5: Take Your Game to the Next Level. Whether you are a rank beginner or have years of experience in social

media marketing, find out how to take your game to a whole new level.

**To join our program today, please email us:**

RamajonCogan
wheresramajon@gmail.com

CatherineCarrigan
catherine@catherinecarrigan.com

# Chapter 10: Who We Are: Catherine Carrigan

Catherine Carrigan is an Amazon No. 1 best selling author and medical intuitive healer.

Catherine became a social media entrepreneur and authorpreneur after the publication of her second book, *What Is Healing? Awaken Your Intuitive Power for Health and Happiness.*

"I started in social media to get the word out for people all over the world who need my work and my books," Catherine Carrigan says. "I discovered that social media can be fun and effective.

"Ramajon Cogan, who has been working with authors for five years, and I put this business together to help you because most author-preneurs and entrepreneurs are not financially successful because they do not have a consistent social media marketing approach.

"Ramajon and I call our system the Game of Social Media.

"Join us today to discover how to rocket your business and books to success by learning how to play our game."

At present, Catherine's Social Authority is 68, which puts her in the top 14.6 percent of Twitter users worldwide. She is consistently among the top 100 Twitter users in Atlanta, Georgia.

Her score on Klout, a broad-based measurement of average influence across Twitter, Facebook,

Google+, Instagram, LinkedIn and Tumblr, is 68. The average Klout score is 40 on a scale of 1 to 100, with the president ranking at 99.

Four of her recent books: *What Is Healing? Awaken Your Intuitive Power for Health and Happiness, Unlimited Energy Now* and *Banish the Blues Now* and *Unlimited Intuition Now,* went to No. 1 on Amazon.

Through the effective use of combining blogging, social media and building a strong social network, Catherine Carrigan's brand identity shows up on page one of Google under search term "medical intuitive." Many of her blog articles have reached the front page of Google for FREE using the social media strategy template that she has created.

Want to find out more about how you can win the Game of Social Media?

Call today to find out how:

CatherineCarrigan

(678)612-8816

catherine@catherinecarrigan.com.

Read about her work on her four websites:

www.catherinecarrigan.com

www.unlimitedenergynow.com

www.whatissocialmediatoday.com

www.healingjewelrystore.com

Here's how to connect with Catherine through the social media:

Twitter:

https://twitter.com/CSCarrigan

Facebook:

https://www.facebook.com/catherinecarriganauthor

Pinterest:

http://www.pinterest.com/carrigan112/

Instagram:

https://www.instagram.com/catherinecarriganauthor/

Youtube:
https://www.youtube.com/channel/UCCvjD3IT R1gKQEyS2JBT3QQ
Tumblr:
https://www.tumblr.com/blog/ccarrigan

Google+:
https://plus.google.com/u/0/115315690318090975674

# Chapter 11: Who We Are: Ramajon Cogan

RamaJon Cogan spent five years working with hundreds of authors as the former director of PublishNow.

During those five years, Rama worked on every aspect of publishing and determined that the reason that most authorpreneurs and entrepreneurs do not succeed financially is because they do not have a strong broad based social media marketing platform.

"I am passionate about helping authors and small business owners succeed," Rama says.

"In the old days, brick and mortar retailers survived based of location, location location. In today's digital age, it's marketing, marketing marketing."

"Catherine Carrigan and I are committed to empowering you to succeed with our new business What Is Social Media Today.

"We have developed a highly successful approach that we call the Game of Social Media.

Our goal is to teach you how to play the game so that you can be successful and bring your business and books to a worldwide audience."

Ramajon is a computer geek, adventurer and renegade mountain biker.

He received his B.A. from University of Wisconsin, Madison, with a major in economics and a minor in organization theory.

His first professional job was as a productivity consultant for ROI Controls Corp. Being the low man on the totem pole, number crunching and basic programming were the rule of the day.

Dropping out and following his dreams to Hawaii, RamaJon had his *Adventures with Hawaiian Hippies and Holymen*.

Since then, RamaJon has been his own boss, owning Rising Sun Natural Foods in Cleveland for 5 years and then riding the energy of the New Age to Sedona and opening Mountain Bike Heaven which established the Sedona Mountain Bike Community and *The Rise of the Gnarly Crew*.

In 2011 RamaJon changed his life from bike rider to book writer; publishing his long awaited book:

*Sedona Mountain Biking: The Rise of the Gnarly Crew* which became an Amazon #1 Bestseller

Shortly thereafter, RamaJon became book writing and publishing coach and consultant for Tom Bird's PublishNow program.

From early Basic and Cobol programming to pioneering the Sedona Mountain Biking community to What Is Social Media Today, RamaJon has been part of technology growth.

RamaJon brings you his jack of all trades down to earth perspective and is Director of Fun for The Game Of Social Media.

RamaJon considers Instagram a social media playground and plays there at:
https://www.instagram.com/tropicallyhip/

You can also check out his website:

http://www.mountainbikeheaven.com/

Join us today and have fun succeeding, winning
over a new audience and making money
Want to find out more about how you can win
the Game of Social Media?

Catherine: catherine@catherinecarrigan.com.

Ramajon: wheresramajon@gmail.com.

What is
# HEALING?

Awaken Your
Intuitive Power for
Health and Happiness

CATHERINE
CARRIGAN

About *What Is Healing? Awaken Your Intuitive Power for Health and Happiness*

In this book, you will:

- Learn how unconditional love can awaken your intuitive gifts.

- Reveal how to open your heart to access your highest intelligence.

- Uncover how to communicate with your angels and spiritual guides.

- Awaken your own psychic abilities.

- Identify the key aspects of a medical intuitive reading.

- Discern how addiction to staying sick can keep you from healing.

- Reveal the blessing behind a mental or physical breakdown.

- Grasp the four key difficulties that lead to health problems.

- Empower your own spiritual growth.

UNLIMITED

ENERGY

NOW

AMAZON #1 BESTSELLER

CATHERINE CARRIGAN

About *Unlimited Energy Now*

Discover the secrets of how you can experience unlimited energy *now:*

- Learn how to operate your body at its very best.

- Master your own energy system.

- Resolve the emotions that drain you.

- Connect to your highest intelligence.

- Inspire yourself to connect more deeply to your infinite, eternal and unwavering support from your soul.

# Banish the Blues
# NOW

# Catherine Carrigan

*Banish the Blues NOW* addresses:

HEALING    DEPRESSION    WITHOUT
DRUGS   using   NATURAL   HEALING
remedies.

Women are more likely than men to take these drugs at every level of severity of depression.

Of those taking antidepressants, 60 percent have taken them for more than 2 years, and 14 percent have taken the drugs for more than 10 years. About 8 percent of persons aged 12 and over with no current depressive symptoms took antidepressant medication.

Despite the widespread acceptance of natural healing methods, from 1988-1994 through 2005-2008, the rate of antidepressant use in the United States among all ages increased nearly 400 percent.

It is my prayer that my new book will be of service in teaching you how to heal depression without drugs, banishing your blues FOR GOOD!

Unlimited Intuition
NOW

Catherine Carrigan

READ *UNLIMITEDINTUITION NOW*
TO DEVELOP YOUR OWN PSYCHIC ABILITIES
SO THAT YOU CAN RECEIVE GUIDANCE FROM
YOUR SOUL.

How you will benefit:

- Pray to open your soul guidance.
- Learn how to read the energy in your. chakras with a pendulum
- Tune in to read your own body.
- Discover how to read the body of another person.
- Discern how much life force is in your food.
- Focus to tell if food is really good for your body.
- Practice how to muscle test yourself.
- Raise your vibration to listen to your angels.
- Get your ego out of the way so you can listen to divine guidance.
- Stay connected with loved ones when you are apart.
- Open your psychic centers of clairaudience, claircognizance, clairsentience and clairvoyance.
- Avoid other people's ego projections to see what's really going on.
- Protect your energy so you feel safe and grounded at all times and in all places.
- Stay out of trouble in dangerous situations.
- Understand how your different psychic gifts actually work.
- Deepen your connection to God and feel supported on all levels.

46344156R00058

Made in the USA
San Bernardino, CA
05 March 2017